Tools

Search

Notes

Discuss

MyReportLinks.com Books

Go!

CIVILIZATIONS OF THE ANCIENT WORLD

ANCIENT CHINA

A MyReportLinks.com Book

NEIL D. BRAMWELL

MyReportLinks.com Books
an imprint of

Enslow Publishers, Inc.
Box 398, 40 Industrial Road
Berkeley Heights, NJ 07922
USA

MyReportLinks.com Books, an imprint of Enslow Publishers, Inc. MyReportLinks®
is a registered trademark of Enslow Publishers, Inc.

Library of Congress Cataloging-in-Publication Data

Bramwell, Neil D., 1932–
  Ancient China / Neil D. Bramwell.
    p. cm. — (Civilizations of the ancient world)
Includes bibliographical references and index.
  ISBN 0-7660-5184-6
  1. China—Juvenile literature. I. Title. II. Series.
  DS706.B66 2004
  931—dc22

                          2003020674

Printed in the United States of America

10 9 8 7 6 5 4 3 2 1

To Our Readers:
Through the purchase of this book, you and your library gain access to the Report Links that specifically back
up this book.
The Publisher will provide access to the Report Links that back up this book and will keep these Report Links
up to date on **www.myreportlinks.com** for three years from the book's first publication date.
We have done our best to make sure all Internet addresses in this book were active and appropriate when we
went to press. However, the author and the Publisher have no control over, and assume no liability for, the
material available on those Internet sites or on other Web sites they may link to.
The usage of the MyReportLinks.com Books Web site is subject to the terms and conditions stated on the
Usage Policy Statement on **www.myreportlinks.com**.
A password may be required to access the Report Links that back up this book. The password is found on the
bottom of page 4 of this book.
Any comments or suggestions can be sent by e-mail to comments@myreportlinks.com or to the address on
the back cover.

Photo Credits: © 1998–2004, TravelChinaGuide.com, p. 9; © Corel Corporation, pp. 22, 30; China
National Tourism Administration, pp. 12, 43; Chinapage.com, p. 41; Clipart.com, pp. 1, 15, 25, 38; Enslow
Publishers, Inc., p. 21; Internet East Asian Sourcebook, pp. 16, 29; Minnesota State University, Mankato,
p. 27; MyReportLinks.com Books, pp. 4, back cover; *National Geographic*.com, pp. 14, 34; Photos.com,
p. 3; Smith College Museum of Ancient Inventions, p. 33; The Metropolitan Museum of Art, p. 19; The
National Gallery of Art, pp. 18, 36; University of Texas, p. 11.

Cover Photos: Bronze mask, Painet Stock Photos; Great Wall, © Corel Corporation; Terra-cotta warriors,
© Fotosearch LLC.

Contents

ANCIENT CHINA

Report Links **4**

Time Line **9**

1   **An Army Protects the First Emperor** **10**

2   **History** **13**

3   **Land, People, and Religion** **20**

4   **Family Life: Education, Food, Clothing, Shelter** **32**

5   **Arts and Cultural Contributions** **38**

6   **Government** **40**

Chapter Notes **45**

Further Reading **47**

Index **48**

MyReportLinks.com Books
Great Books, Great Links, Great for Research!

The Report Links listed on the following four pages can save you hours of research time by **instantly** bringing you to the best Web sites relating to your report topic.

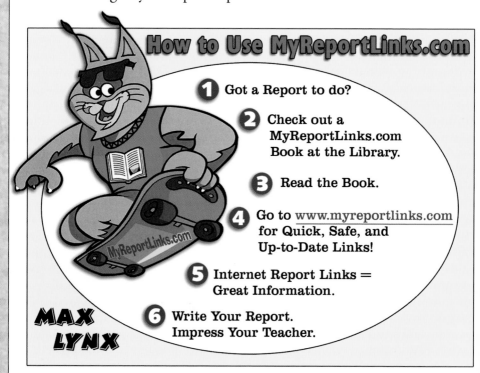

How to Use MyReportLinks.com

1 Got a Report to do?

2 Check out a MyReportLinks.com Book at the Library.

3 Read the Book.

4 Go to www.myreportlinks.com for Quick, Safe, and Up-to-Date Links!

5 Internet Report Links = Great Information.

6 Write Your Report. Impress Your Teacher.

MAX LYNX

The pre-evaluated Web sites are your links to source documents, photographs, illustrations, and maps. They also provide links to dozens—even hundreds—of Web sites about your report subject.

MyReportLinks.com Books and the MyReportLinks.com Web site save you time and make report writing easier than ever!

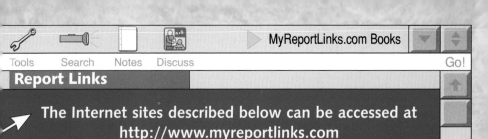
Report Links

➤ The Internet sites described below can be accessed at
http://www.myreportlinks.com

*EDITOR'S CHOICE

▶History of China: A Table of Contents
This Web site offers a wealth of information about China's history,
including its ancient dynasties.

*EDITOR'S CHOICE

▶Museum of Qin Terra-Cotta Warriors and Horses
This site offers a look inside the Museum of the Qin Terra-cotta
Warriors and Horses, in Shaanxi province, which features thousands
of life-size figures found near the tomb of an ancient emperor.

*EDITOR'S CHOICE

▶China: A Country Study
A comprehensive political, social, and cultural history of China
is to be found in this Library of Congress Web site.

*EDITOR'S CHOICE

▶China
This site offers a useful time line of Chinese dynasties and rulers
from ancient times through the imperial era.

*EDITOR'S CHOICE

▶Exploring Ancient World Cultures
An introduction to ancient cultures is offered with this site.
In particular, Taoism and its founder are discussed.

*EDITOR'S CHOICE

▶Chinese History
This Web site provides an abundance of information about the
dynasties, or ruling families, who reigned throughout much of
China's long history.

The Internet sites described below can be accessed at http://www.myreportlinks.com

▶**Ancient Chinese Pottery and Bronze**

Explore the arts of China at this Smithsonian Web site. Here you can learn about different techniques used in making bronzes, pottery, and ceramics.

▶**Ancient Writings from the Ruins of Yin**

At the Ancient Writings from the Ruins of Yin Web site, visitors will learn about the earliest known writing in China, which consisted of inscriptions on the bones and shells of animals.

▶**China the Beautiful**

This Web site from China provides a look at a variety of topics, including Chinese culture and history, and includes links to a variety of sites.

▶**The Chinese Calendar**

This site offers exhibits of Chinese calendars through the ages. The first calenders appeared during the Shang dynasty.

▶**Chinese Cultural Studies: Concise Political History of China**

This Web site offers a brief but informative history of China, the world's oldest continuing civilization.

▶**Chinese Myths and Fantasies**

Some of the myths and stories of China that have existed since ancient times and are still known to Chinese children are presented on this site.

▶**Compass, China**

On this Web site you can view an early compass that was made in China during the period of the Han Dynasty.

▶**Confucius and the Scholars**

This *Atlantic Monthly* article presents two interesting recent studies that shed new light on Confucius and his influence in Chinese society.

Report Links

The Internet sites described below can be accessed at http://www.myreportlinks.com

►Exploring Chinese History

At the Exploring Chinese History Web site you can learn about ancient China, its culture, and its political life.

►The Han Dynasty

This Metropolitan Museum of Art page includes a brief history of life in ancient China under the Han dynasty and provides examples of Han art.

►Internet East Asian History Sourcebook

The Internet East Asian History Sourcebook is a site that offers a comprehensive history of China as well as many links to other sites.

►The Mausoleum of Qin Shi Huangdi

Learn about the mausoleum of Qin Shi Huangdi located near the ancient city of Xi'an and the discovery of his tomb in 1974.

►*National Geographic:* Great Wall of China

This *National Geographic* site offers a photographic journey to one of the world's great wonders: the Great Wall of China, part of China's ancient and enduring heritage.

►The New Story of China's Ancient Past

This *National Geographic* site tells the story of artifacts unearthed in China that date back to the Shang dynasty.

►Qin Dynasty

This Metropolitan Museum of Art site offers a brief overview of ancient China during the Qin dynasty and includes a map of Qin lands.

►Religion

At the Chinese-American Culture Bridge Center Web site you can explore some of the major religions and philosophies, including Buddhism, Confucianism, and Taoism, that have shaped Chinese culture.

Report Links

The Internet sites described below can be accessed at http://www.myreportlinks.com

▶**Secrets of the Lost Empires: China Bridge**

This PBS Web site explores the history of China Bridge, the effort by a team of NOVA scientists to build a bridge like those found in ancient China.

▶**The Silk Road**

At this Web site you will learn about Xi'an, an ancient capital of China, and the Silk Road, which linked China to other lands through the silk trade.

▶**Silk Road Encounters**

The Silk Road Encounters Web site provides information about Chinese history, religion, art, trade, and music. You will also find useful maps and art exhibitions.

▶**The Splendors of Imperial China: Treasures from the National Palace Museum, Taipei**

A treasure trove of Chinese art including paintings, pottery, and other decorative pieces can be found at the Asian Art Museum of San Francisco Web site.

▶**Taoism**

This site offers a brief description of Taoism, an ancient Chinese philosophy that still influences Chinese culture today.

▶**Teaching the Golden Age of Chinese Archaeology**

At the National Gallery of Art Web site you can explore artifacts from late prehistoric China, the Bronze Age, Chu and other cultures, and the Imperial era.

▶**Travel China Guide**

At the Travel China Guide Web site you can explore the Great Wall, the Museum of the Terra-cotta Warriors, the Forbidden City, the Silk Road, and many other interesting places linked to China's history.

▶**Visions of China**

Explore China at the Visions of China Web site, which includes information about China's history and archaeological finds that have been unearthed in China.

Any comments? Contact us: **comments@myreportlinks.com**

Dynasty	Years of Rule	Major Events
Xia	c.1994–c.1523 B.C.	Agriculture developed; bronze used
Shang	c.1523–1027 B.C.	First calendar; uniform writing
Zhou	1027–221 B.C.	Age of Confucius; use of money and iron; first written laws
	Spring and Autumn Period 771–476 B.C.	Growth of independent states
	Warring States Period 475–221 B.C.	Warfare with bows, spears, halberds
Qin	221–207 B.C.	China unified; Great Wall begun; roads built; written Chinese standardized
Han	206 B.C.– A.D. 220 *Western Han* 206 B.C.– A.D. 8 *Wang Mang* A.D. 8–23 *Eastern Han* A.D. 23–220	Central rule strengthened; Buddhism introduced; postal system; taxes imposed

A gourd-shaped jar from the Zhou dynasty. ▽

Chapter 1

AN ARMY PROTECTS THE FIRST EMPEROR

In Xi'an, a city in the Shaanxi province of northwestern China, thousands of soldiers, perhaps more than seven thousand, stand in formation in three underground pits. They are ready to defend their emperor, whose body lies entombed nearby, from any enemy. They have remained in formation, ready for battle, for over two thousand years. The soldiers are life-size, ranging in height from 5 feet 8 inches to 6 feet 2.5 inches, and are made of terra-cotta, a form of baked clay. Each soldier's features are unique to him, as if modeled from different individuals. Their weapons, longbows, spears, battle-axes, and halberds, which combine spear and battle-ax, are stored nearby. These soldiers are known as the terra-cotta warriors, and the 14,000-square-foot museum where they reside is one of China's most-visited cultural sites.

The emperor's soldiers are arrayed in formations according to their function in battle, ready to ward off attackers from any direction. Some soldiers are in kneeling positions while others are standing. There are also seventy-four full-size chariots, drawn by four horses each, in which other soldiers or officers ride. There are, as well, nearly six hundred life-size Mongolian ponies.

Each soldier wears a uniform whose color corresponds to his rank. The colors are purple, blue, green, yellow, red, and orange. The uniforms range from heavy knee-length tunics and cloth leg wrappings to armor made from hundreds of pieces of iron shaped like fish scales.[1]

e Mausoleum of Qin Shi Huangdi - Microsoft Internet Explorer

Edit   View   Favorites   Tools   Help

ress http://www.utexas.edu/courses/wilson/ant304/biography/arybios98/smithbio.html   Go

Recently discovered in 1974 by Chinese peasants who were drilling a well, the tomb of Qin Shi Huangdi proved to be one of the greatest archaeological finds in both historical importance and in sheer physical bulk. Archaeologists were uncertain when the excavations began of the great magnitude of this site. The although the tomb itself is, according to legend, very elaborate and beautiful, the center piece of Shi Huangdi's mausoleum is the terra-cotta army of approximately 8,000 life-sized men and horses. Individually sculpted of 3 inch thick terra-cotta clay, each soldier and horse is unique, each with its own style of dress (the mineral paints used to cover the figures in bright, gay colors have since dissolved), weaponry, and facial expressions. Grouped into a specific military formation with crouching crossbowmen and bowmen at the point, archers at the flanks, large groups of infantry, chariots and cavalry, and a final guard of heavily

Internet

▲ The terra-cotta warriors who have been guarding the tomb of Emperor Shi Huangdi were discovered only thirty years ago by some Chinese farmers who were drilling a well.

The emperor's tomb that these soldiers have been guarding for over two thousand years took over thirty years to build and is located west of the burial chambers of the army. The tomb itself has not yet been excavated, but according to Chinese legend, it is supposed to be a replica of his empire, with rivers of quicksilver (mercury) and many marvels, including death traps for any tomb robbers.[2]

Shi Huangdi (Qin Shi Huang), the emperor who had this army buried to protect himself for all time, founded the first empire of China in 221 B.C. His conquests united the many states that had fought each other-for years in

▲ *Some of the terra-cotta warriors and their horses guarding the First Emperor's tomb.*

China. He called himself "August Sovereign," the name that all emperors of China used afterward. He was the founder of the Qin dynasty. Dynasties are periods of rule by members of the same family, and most of China's long history is divided into dynasties, beginning in about 1994 B.C. with the Xia dynasty and lasting until A.D. 1911, with the end of the Qing dynasty. The political system of the three earliest dynasties, the Xia, Shang, and Zhou, was a feudal system. The dynasties that followed, beginning with the Qin, were centralized empires.

HISTORY

China is the birthplace of the world's oldest continuous civilization, with a written history that began 3,500 years ago. Humans have lived in what is now China long before history was recorded, however. Archaeologists have uncovered evidence that shows humans who made tools were living in China at least twelve thousand years ago. Humans lived partly underground, in dwellings dug into the earth and roofed over. Pigs and dogs had been domesticated and pottery making had been learned.

▶ The Xia, Shang, and Zhou Dynasties

By 2205 B.C., China consisted of a number of small states that, according to tradition, were conquered and united by the Xia dynasty, which ruled from 1994 to 1523 B.C. From that dynasty until A.D. 1911, the history of China is the story of the rise and fall of dynasties, which usually came to power by conquest. The first historical dynasty is the Shang dynasty, which dates from 1523 to 1027 B.C.

The Shang kings were powerful rulers, with great armies at their command. They could send from three thousand to five thousand soldiers into battle at a time. The soldiers in these armies used bronze weapons that included a complex bow and arrow and a halberd. The army was driven to the scene of battle by chariots and would then dismount to begin fighting.

The Shang dynasty was overthrown by the Zhou dynasty, whose rule lasted from 1027 to 221 B.C. Under the

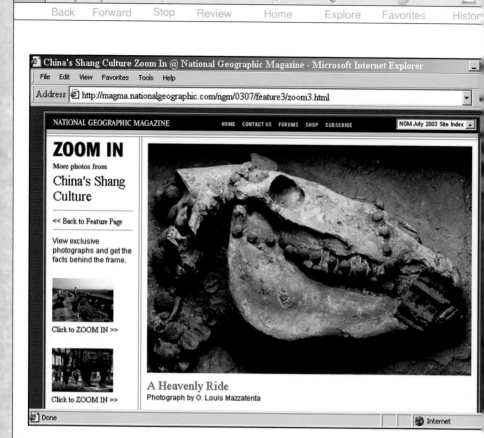

A Heavenly Ride
Photograph by O. Louis Mazzatenta

Archaeologists who excavated a Shang tomb in 1971 found this horse's skull studded with bronze decorations left from the horse's bridle.

Zhou dynasty, the government extended its control into north and south China by conquest and planned settlements. In the later period of Zhou rule, the central government's authority became less strong. This period, known as the Spring and Autumn period, is marked by the growth of independent states. These states paid only a small allegiance to the central government.

▶ The Warring States Period

By 475 B.C., the independent states began fighting each other so often that the period from 475 to 221 has come to be called the Warring States period. Its end also marked the end of the Zhou dynasty.[1] Warfare was waged with the composite bow, whose arrows were made with bronze or clay points. Other weapons used during this period of warfare included bronze spears, battle-axes, and halberds.

▷ The End of War: The Qin Dynasty

In 221 B.C., peace was restored to the empire when China became united under the Qin dynasty and the First Emperor. During the Qin dynasty, written Chinese became standardized, and the vast empire was united by a vast system of roads and canals.

Despite its lasting influence, the Qin dynasty ruled for only fifteen years. It ended with the murder of the First Emperor's son in 207 B.C. Rebellion and civil war

▲ A jade water container created during the Han dynasty.

had broken out even before that event, however. From these warring groups emerged a farmer who lost every battle but his last one. Liu Pang, also known as Han Gaozu, the first commoner to rule China, became the first emperor of the Han dynasty.[2]

The Han Dynasty

The Han dynasty continued the rule of China under a powerful central government. The empire was divided into fourteen commanderies and ten kingdoms ruled by the emperor's sons or nobles he appointed. The powerful bureaucracy that had been set up by the Qin dynasty was expanded to reinforce the central government's control.

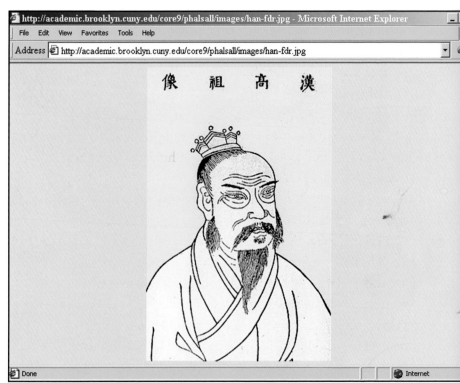

http://academic.brooklyn.cuny.edu/core9/phalsall/images/han-fdr.jpg - Microsoft Internet Explorer

File   Edit   View   Favorites   Tools   Help

Address http://academic.brooklyn.cuny.edu/core9/phalsall/images/han-fdr.jpg

像　祖　高　漢

Done   Internet

▲ *Liu Pang was China's first emperor to come from a common background. He founded the Han dynasty in 206 B.C.*

It was during this period that government inspectors were sent to all regions of the empire. They reported back to the central office in the capital on the conditions and the administration in each of the inspector's districts. The inspectors communicated with the capital via a postal system, which was set up along the main highways that linked the empire.

The money to run the government came from taxes. A land tax and a head tax were imposed on the population. State income also came from taxes paid on silk and revenues that came from government-owned industries, such as the salt and iron industries.

The Han dynasty continued its rule from 206 B.C. until A.D. 220 except for a fifteen-year period from A.D. 8 to A.D. 23. During those years, Wang Mang's Xin dynasty ruled China. Han rule is therefore divided into the Former Han or Western Han (206 B.C. to A.D. 8) and the Later Han or Eastern Han (A.D. 23 to 220).

The Han dynasty had vast armies at its command and was able to expand the empire a great deal. In 137 B.C., the Han emperor sent an army of three hundred thousand men to Mongolia. Within ten years, the Han controlled Inner Mongolia. The dynasty then took control of Korea between 109 and 106 B.C. By 82 B.C. the Han dynasty had extended China's borders to Burma.

The armies of the Han dynasty were made up of farmers and professional soldiers as well as mercenary troops recruited from north of the empire's borders. At the age of thirty, every man in the empire had to enroll and serve one year in the army. For those who served on the frontiers of the empire, service was permanent.

However, as powerful as the Han armies were, they were never able to conquer the nomad tribes north of

China, beyond what became known as the Great Wall. That wall was begun by the First Emperor and was expanded under later dynasties to keep out invading nomads from China's north. It failed to do so. Invasion and attack from north of the wall was a frequent threat in ancient China until northern tribes finally succeeded in conquering China.

Dynasties rose and fell in the centuries after the Han dynasty and China's conquest by the Mongols and the Qing dynasty. But the powerful central state created by the Qin dynasty, which was expanded and strengthened by

Gilt bronze human-shaped lamp - Microsoft Internet Explorer

File   Edit   View   Favorites   Tools   Help

Address http://www.nga.gov/exhibitions/china1999/307_137.htm

Gilt bronze human-shaped lamp, Western Han Dynasty (c. 113 B.C.)
Hebei Provincial Museum, Shijiazhuang

Done   Internet

▲ *The prized possessions of powerful people in ancient China were often buried with them. This gilt bronze lamp in the shape of a kneeling man was found in the tomb of Prince Liu Sheng, buried in 113 B.C.*

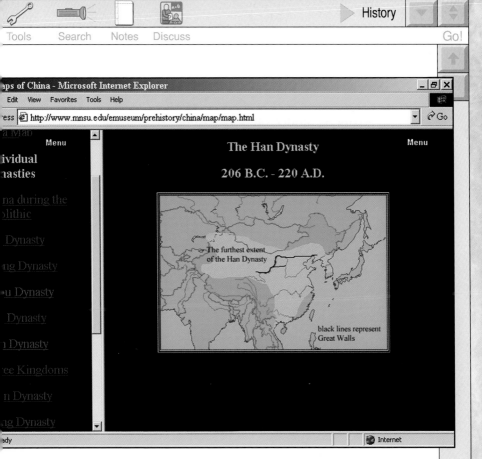

The Han Dynasty

206 B.C. - 220 A.D.

The furthest extent
of the Han Dynasty

black lines represent
Great Walls

▲ *The black lines on this map of the Han dynasty represent the Great Wall.*

the Han dynasty, remained in place until the end of the empire in 1911. The concept of a powerful and virtuous emperor ruling through a vast bureaucracy under strict law and strongly influenced by philosophies of the time was adapted and used by the succeeding dynasties.

19

LAND, PEOPLE, AND RELIGION

China is the largest country in the world in population and the fourth-largest in area. China's east coast is bordered by three seas, the Yellow Sea, the East China Sea, and the South China Sea, which are all part of the Pacific Ocean. China's northern border reaches Mongolia and Russia while to the south, China reaches North Vietnam. To the west, China's major neighbor is India.

Northern China was and is cold and dry, suitable only for the cultivation of wheat or barley and millet and some pasturage for horses and cattle. Most important to the people in the north of China is the deposit by wind and dust storms of a rich, fertile soil known as loess. Loess deposits, which can be hundreds of feet deep, provided shelter for the ancient Chinese, since they were able to dig homes in them. Southern China was warm and tropical in part and suitable for the cultivation of rice, tea, and mulberry trees whose leaves provided the food for silkworms. Those silkworms provided the Chinese with the material to make silk, which was also produced in other regions. Silk has been an important material throughout Chinese history.

▷ Major Rivers

There are more than five hundred rivers in China, but two, the Yellow River (Huang He) and the Yangzi River (Chang Jiang), are of greatest importance in Chinese history. The Yellow River runs for approximately 2,700 miles from the Kunlun Mountains in western China to the Bo Hai, an

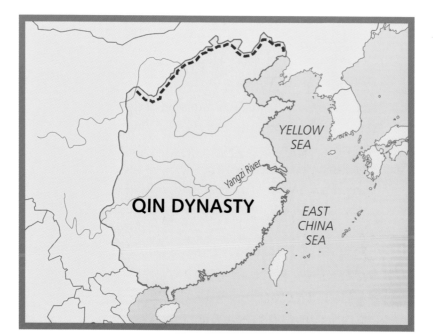

▲ The Yangzi River has always played a major role in Chinese history. The Zhou dynasty (also spelled Chou) arose in the Yangzi River Valley.

arm of the Yellow Sea, in the east, but its course has changed—or been changed—through the centuries. The Yellow River has overflowed its banks countless times in China's long history, causing flooding over thousands of miles. That flooding has led to a vast deposit of loess from which the early centers of China grew.[1]

China's longest river is the Yangzi, flowing 3,200 miles from the Tibetan plateau to the East China Sea. Unlike the Yellow River, the Yangzi is navigable. Large ships can navigate the Yangzi for up to 1,000 miles from the coast to the interior of China, after which smaller ships can travel an additional 600 miles.[2] Throughout China's history, the Yangzi has been a highway of communication, commerce, and trade from China's coast deep into its interior. China

is roughly divided into north and south regions by a line drawn midway between the Yellow River and the Yangzi.

▶ Farming and Mining

Agriculture was the main occupation of the Chinese under the Shang kings and through the Han Empire. There were few cities except those established as capitals by the kings and emperors or local centers for the administration of the government. Most of the population lived in small towns and villages whose inhabitants were connected by family or clan ties.

While the majority of the population consisted of farmers, there were significant numbers of skilled artisans such as bronze makers, potters, and even makers of musical

▲ According to legend, the use of tea was discovered by Emperor Shennong of China about 2737 B.C. The earliest known mention of tea appeared in Chinese literature of about A.D. 350. These workers are cultivating tea in present-day China.

instruments such as bells and ocarinas, which are oval wind instruments.[3] Beginning in the Qin dynasty and expanded under the Han dynasty, there was a large bureaucracy of government officials.

Farmers paid rent to the government in the form of crops or labor to live on the land they farmed. They were also forced to donate their time to work on dikes, roads, and public buildings. Forced labor was also used to build defensive walls of rammed earth with the hardness of cement around the cities and larger towns. There were small numbers of merchants who lived in the capital cities or traveled the countryside.

By the Shang dynasty, 1523 B.C. to 1027 B.C., bronze was in wide use, and the Shang kings used chariots and weapons of bronze. Iron, first cast in 513 B.C., was in general use by 400 B.C., mainly in agriculture. With the invention of the bellows, steel was being produced in China by the second century B.C.

▶ Early Writing

The history of Shang rule is derived from vast numbers of bones and tortoise shells discovered in Anyang, one of the Shang king's capitals. The bones and shells are inscribed with questions asked by the kings and answers given by specialists practiced in the art of interpreting the cracks and markings in the bones and shells that were produced by heating them. This practice was known as divination. Oracles, people who were considered to have a special wisdom and the ability to foretell the future, would read the cracks in the bones and answer questions asked of them by government officials. Those questions might be about almost anything, because it is believed that the Shang were highly superstitious. But they probably asked questions about the worship of ancestors,

what military actions should be taken, and whether those actions would be successful.

In addition to the bones and tortoise shells, official accounts are also derived from writings on bamboo and wood. The existence of these written records shows that writing was already highly developed by the Shang period. Its origin in China is still unknown.[4]

▶ Religion

Religion in China by the time of the Shang dynasty was made up of many elements. Ancestor worship was one of the many features of early Chinese religion. Ancestor worship was limited to the wealthier classes until the period of the Han dynasty. Farmers and their families devoted their worship mainly to local deities for fertility of farm and family. The various deities were honored with ceremonies, and sacrifices were carried out by heads of families. As society became more organized, state officials, including the king, performed certain rites and ceremonies.

There was no official class of priests in ancient China.[5] But worship was conducted with the help of an individual known as a shaman. Shamans enlisted the help of certain animals who were thought to have a special connection with the ancestors whose advice and assistance were being sought.[6] Kings and emperors also assumed the role of shaman.

In the Shang dynasty, religion differed from place to place, each area having its own local deity. Many deities were the same gods with different names. Ultimately the government made one god, Shangdi, the Lord on High, the official deity. Kings and ministers were worshiped after their deaths because it was believed that they could approach Shangdi, the supreme god, on behalf of the common people.

In 1027 B.C., the Zhou dynasty conquered the Shang dynasty. Under Zhou rule, human sacrifice was officially forbidden.[7] Until then, humans as well as animals including cattle, dogs, and pigs were sacrificed to the gods. Most of the humans sacrificed were prisoners of war. But villagers may have fought and captured people from other villages for this human sacrifice.[8] Human sacrifice was also made during the burial ceremonies of the kings. The burial of the thousands of terra-cotta soldiers near the First Emperor's tomb may have been a substitute for the burial of actual soldiers.

▲ *The teachings of Confucius (right) have influenced Chinese life and thought for centuries.*

A significant part of ancient Chinese religion was based on certain philosophies that were more concerned with human relationships than with a person's relationship to a personal god. These philosophies addressed the question of how to organize society and a person's relationship with others for his or her own good and the greater good of the state.

▶ Philosophies: Legalism, Confucianism, and Taoism

Ancient China was home to three schools of philosophy that have affected thought and behavior throughout Chinese history. These schools of philosophy are known as Legalism, Confucianism, and Taoism.

▶ Legalism

Legalism is the belief that society must be built on law and serve the interest of the state. Legalism continued to exert a strong influence up to modern times and was particularly powerful in its effect on the governments of the Qin and Han dynasties.

As Legalism was practiced, judges were supposed to correctly identify a crime and its punishment as specifically set forth in law. Strict law must define the crime and its punishment and not be subject to interpretation by the judge or other individuals.[9]

Underlying Legalism is the belief in a powerful centralized state run by officials who are appointed by a ruler who must be obeyed without question. The law, which could not be questioned, had to be made known to the public and administered according to specific rules and regulations.

By the time of the Han dynasty, the law was supposed to be applied equally to all people, commoners as well as the nobility. But by the late Han dynasty, there were distinctions based on rank in how the law was applied.

Confucianism

Confucius (551–479 B.C.), whose teachings led to a school of philosophy, lived during the second half of the Zhou dynasty (1027–221 B.C.) The Zhou were the conquerors of the Shang. The teachings of Confucius have had a profound effect on China throughout its history. Confucianism became the official philosophy in the Han

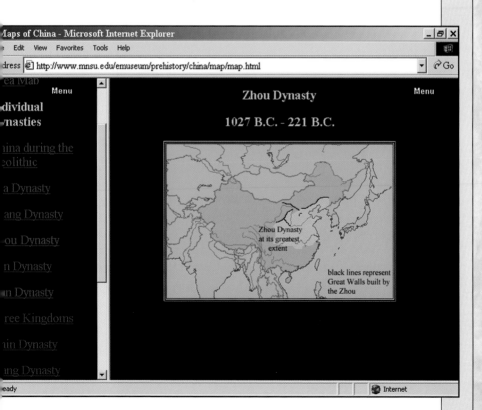

Maps of China - Microsoft Internet Explorer

Edit   View   Favorites   Tools   Help

dress http://www.mnsu.edu/emuseum/prehistory/china/map/map.html   Go

Menu   **Zhou Dynasty**   Menu

1027 B.C. - 221 B.C.

Zhou Dynasty
at its greatest
extent

black lines represent
Great Walls built by
the Zhou

dividual
nasties

ina during the
olithic

a Dynasty

ang Dynasty

ou Dynasty

n Dynasty

n Dynasty

ree Kingdoms

in Dynasty

ng Dynasty

eady   Internet

This map shows the lands of the Zhou dynasty at its greatest extent.

27

dynasty. It dominated Chinese thought to the end of the empire, in 1911.

Little is known about Confucius's life. Modern scholars base most of what they do know on a collection of his sayings and stories about his life collected by his followers that were written down after Confucius's death. This collection, called the *Analects*, was added to over the centuries by other writers of philosophy.

Confucius taught that man's relationships with others begins in the family, from father to son, elder brother to younger brother. Good relationships within the family, beginning with those between father and son, extend to one's relationship to strangers and finally to the relationship between the ruler and his subjects. Confucius did not teach about a personal god or even promote a doctrine of religion. He did include in his teachings the doctrine of the Mandate of Heaven and the belief in Destiny. The Mandate of Heaven states that Heaven calls for the most virtuous man to be China's ruler. If that man loses his virtue, he will in turn lose the Mandate of Heaven, and his dynasty will be overthrown. Destiny, beyond human control, dictated one's condition in life by determining a person's wealth and health.[10]

Belief in the Mandate of Heaven and Destiny was central to Confucius's teaching because it meant that people should behave in a way that fit in with their position in life. Confucius did not believe that humans should lead passive lives, however. Instead, he urged people to devote themselves to living a moral life that followed the Way of Heaven as taught by the ancient sages.[11]

According to Confucius, every man had the potential and duty to reach the same state of virtue, or level of goodness, that the ancient sages had achieved. While acknowledging that Destiny was in control of the human

condition, Confucius believed that humans had the free will to choose to live good lives.

In Confucian thought, virtue could only be achieved within a carefully ordered society, which could only come about when selfishness and greed were overcome by all people within that society. The way to virtue was by achieving benevolence, which happened when people considered others before themselves.[12] In order to know virtue, it was the duty of every man to study the ancient sages, considered the source of all virtue. People were able to gain knowledge about these sages by studying books, especially those known as the *Wu Jing* (Wu Ching), or Five Classics.

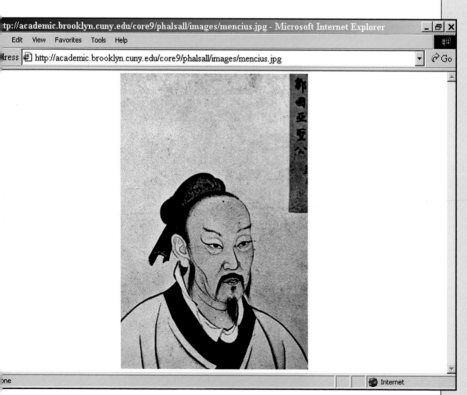

tp://academic.brooklyn.cuny.edu/core9/phalsall/images/mencius.jpg - Microsoft Internet Explorer

Edit   View   Favorites   Tools   Help

ress http://academic.brooklyn.cuny.edu/core9/phalsall/images/mencius.jpg   ▼ Go

one   Internet

▲ *Mengzi, more commonly known as Mencius, was born in the ancient state of Ch'ao, now part of Shandong province. His philosophical writings are considered second only to those of Confucius.*

One of those books, the *Book of Changes*, includes ancient Chinese beliefs about the universe. Another book, the *Book of Rituals*, describes the rules governing all behavior between people. It also describes rites and rituals, including religious ceremonies such as those honoring ancestors.[13]

Mencius (or Mengzi), who lived from 371 to 289 B.C., expanded upon Confucius's teachings. Mencius taught that humans are basically good, but that goodness must be strengthened by practicing rites and rituals. That practice allowed one's goodness to overcome the constant threat of selfishness, considered part of human nature.

▷ Taoism

A philosopher who lived at the same time as Confucius was the father of a very different school of thought. His teachings were followed by many during the Han dynasty

▲ *The Li River winds its way past the mountains of Guilin, an ancient city founded in 214 B.C.*

even though Confucianism was the official philosophy. This philosopher, Lao Zi (Lao Tzu), was born in the sixth century B.C. and was acquainted with Confucius. His philosophy, known as Taoism, is contained in the *Lao Zi* (*Lao Tzu*), or *Daodejing* (*Tao-te Ching*). The *Lao Zi*, which translates as "Classic of the Way and Virtue," is written in parables and verse. It calls for humans to live in natural harmony with the Tao, or Dao, which is considered a cosmic unity that underlies all things. Taoism, unlike Confucianism, teaches that the best government is the one that governs the least.[14] The less people strive, the less the government interferes, the happier all will be. Taoism is based on one's acceptance of his or her natural state. In Taoism, striving to move ahead in society is considered harmful.

Taoism also opposed the practice of the rites and ceremonies that were practiced by the followers of Confucius. According to tradition, in a meeting between Confucius and Lao Zi, Lao Zi implied that the rites were only the words of dead men and therefore useless.[15]

Like Confucianism, Taoism sought order in one's personal life as well as in the state. But unlike Confucianism, Taoism taught that the ruler must avoid actions such as honoring individuals or creating items that could lead to desire. A passage from the *Daodejing* makes this quite plain.

> There is no crime greater than having too many desires;
> There is no disaster greater than not being content;
> There is no misfortune greater than being covetous.[16]

China was, and is, a land of many different cultures. One reason why Chinese civilization has endured can be traced to the beliefs of its people and the teachings of its philosophers.

FAMILY LIFE: EDUCATION, FOOD, CLOTHING, SHELTER

In ancient China, most families lived on farms. The ancient Chinese farm was generally small, only about fifteen acres. All the members of a family worked on a farm. Under the Zhou dynasty, certain sections of a farmer's land were set aside for the nobility. The noble's land was worked by serfs, who were bound under the feudal system to work on a farm but did not own the land. They were subject to the will of the landowner. Farming was hard work, as farmers' tools at the time were mostly made of bone, wood, and stone. With the unification of China under the Qin dynasty, however, feudalism was abolished, people could own land, and individuals were taxed by the government.

▷ The Development of the Calendar

It was essential for a farmer to know when to begin planting his crops. One of the important functions of the emperor was to inform the farmer of the proper time to begin planting. During the Shang dynasty, the development of a calendar was already under way. It was the ancient Chinese who developed the first calendar. In it, a week consisted of ten days, and each day was measured by ten "Heavenly Stems" and twelve "Earthly Branches," in a recurring cycle of sixty days.

By 104 B.C., during the Han dynasty, the four seasons as we now know them were first fixed according to a calendar based on the spring and fall equinoxes and summer and winter solstices. Under Emperor Wang Mang, who ruled

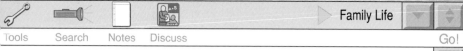

Compass, China, 220 BCE

by Susan Silverman AC

liest records show a spoon shaped compass made of lodestone or magnetite ore, referred
s a "South-pointer" dating back to sometime during the Han Dynasty (2nd century BCE

🌐 Internet

🔺 *A spoon-shaped compass made of lodestone was developed in China
in the second century B.C., during the Han dynasty.*

from A.D. 8 to 23 after overthrowing the Han dynasty, the
year was calculated to consist of just over 365 days.

▷ Clay, Cloth, and Other Early Materials

The ancient Chinese became skilled in the firing of clay
to produce a hard pottery similar to porcelain. Metal at
the time was too scarce and valuable in China to be used
except for coins and weapons. Pottery was a useful substitute for metal, particularly for storing things.

Plant fibers such as hemp were used to make cloth.
Wool came into use under the Zhou dynasty. Silk was
already an important product under the Shang dynasty.

Silk was expensive and particularly important for robes worn in official ceremonies. Silk became the chief export under the Han dynasty, both as gifts to foreign rulers and in trade. Silk in the Han dynasty was exported throughout central Asia, to northern India, and farther west throughout the Roman Empire.[1] The trade route used to transport silk became known as the Silk Road.

▶ The Ancient Chinese Home

In the capital city, houses were made of stone and mud, dried or baked into bricks. Homes for the wealthy were built of wood with roofs supported by pillars resting on

China's Shang Culture Zoom In @ National Geographic Magazine - Microsoft Internet Explorer

File   Edit   View   Favorites   Tools   Help

Address http://magma.nationalgeographic.com/ngm/0307/feature3/zoom6.html

More photos from
China's Shang Culture

<< Back to Feature Page

View exclusive photographs and get the facts behind the frame.

Click to ZOOM IN >>

Click to ZOOM IN >>

Internet

▲ *This 3,500-year-old vessel known as a jue, which dates from the Shang period, probably held wine made from millet or other grains.*

stone or bronze bases. Most homes, except for those of the wealthy, were a place of both family life and work.

In some areas of the countryside, homes were carved out of the sides of mountains or dug deep into the thick compact loess, deposits of silt or clay, for insulation against the cold in the winter and the heat of the summer. Rectangular or oval homes had roofs that were thatched with reeds or straw, with their lower levels set deep in the ground. Housing above the ground appears to have become commonplace around the period of the Warring States, from 475 to 221 B.C., which preceded the Qin dynasty.[2]

Food in Ancient China

Food preparation as art began in China more than three thousand years ago. The foods eaten and prepared by the people of ancient China were as varied as the regions themselves. Chinese cuisine was, and remains, an important part of Chinese culture, and in ancient times, cooking was considered an activity that distinguished civilizations from groups of savages. That food and cooking were important to the ancient Chinese can be seen in a legend about Tang, an emperor of the Shang dynasty, who chose a famous chef, Yi Yen, to be his prime minister. Records also show that more than two thousand people who were on the staff of the imperial palace during the Western Zhou dynasty were kept busy preparing food for the emperor and his wife.[3]

Chinese cuisine is believed to have originated in the Shang period, and it is during this time that historians believe the Chinese mastered the techniques of steaming, stir-frying, and deep-frying that are still used to prepare Chinese food. Rice and wheat were staples, but a balanced diet, considered important for both physical and spiritual well-being, contained vegetables and fruits as well as meat

and fish. The upper classes were able to enjoy a wide variety of meat, including horse, cow, chicken, pig, sheep, and deer, while fish was often the best that commoners could get.

Recent archaeological findings of ancient bronze wares have shed light on what the ancient Chinese ate, since these vessels have been found with food remains. They also show how the ancient Chinese prepared their food. The ding was the most important bronze vessel used to cook meat. It could be either round, with three legs, or rectangular, with four legs, and was elevated to allow a fire underneath. Rice was usually cooked in a li, which had hollow, pouchlike legs that held water. The other main

Shi Qiang bronze vessel (pan) - Microsoft Internet Explorer

File   Edit   View   Favorites   Tools   Help

Address http://www.nga.gov/exhibitions/china1999/423_081.htm

Shi Qiang bronze vessel (pan), Middle Western Zhou Dynasty (end of tenth century B.C.)
Zhouyuan Administrative Office of Cultural Relics, Fufeng

Done   Internet

 This bronze vessel, known as a pan, dates from the middle Western Zhou period, around the end of the tenth century B.C. It was not used for cooking, however, but was a piece made to honor ancestors and important rulers.

kind of cooking vessel was the yan, which was used to steam foods. It had pouchlike legs like a li and an upper part like the top of a ding, but a rack was connected to its base so that the food could be cooked by steam. The Chinese practice of cutting foods into bite-size pieces during preparation, rather than at the dinner table, began during this period and has continued to this day.

Education for the Wealthy

In ancient China, many farmers taught their sons farming, mothers taught their daughters household skills, and craftsmen taught their children and their apprentices their crafts, but roles within families were not always so tied to gender. Formal education was limited to those in wealthy families who could afford tutors. It was not until the age of Confucius, 551 B.C. to 479 B.C., that mass education began in ancient China. By 165 B.C., written examinations were being given to select government officials.[4] In 124 B.C., an imperial academy was created for the study of Confucian texts. Fifty students attended the academy. This system of government-sponsored academies was greatly expanded later under the Han dynasty.

In these academies, students memorized the texts of books that were written on wooden tablets, thin sheets of bamboo, or lengths of silk. These books were texts on medicine and warfare and collections of poetry and philosophy. Students were not permitted to give their own interpretation of the texts.[5] There were no gym classes or recess. Students studied from early morning to late afternoon. Discipline was strict and included beatings. The schools were mainly for the education of government workers and reflected the thinking that the government wanted to promote. Successful students were then enrolled in government service.

Chapter 5 ▶

ARTS AND CULTURAL CONTRIBUTIONS

The oldest Chinese art that has survived from thousands of years ago is in the form of pottery and bronze. By the time of the Shang dynasty, brilliant white earthenware vessels were being fired, or made in kilns. They were decorated by patterns painted onto the surface of the vessel. China's achievement in the art of pottery is considered among the finest in human history.

▶ Bronzes, Pottery, and Paintings

During the Shang dynasty, bronze vessels, statues, and even bells were made and are considered among the finest ever produced anywhere in the world. The bronze vessels were mainly used for religious ceremonies. They were decorated

◀ *This landscape painting on silk was created between 1279 and 960 B.C.*

with pictures of birds and other animals, particularly water buffalo sporting tiger's teeth. In the Han dynasty, bronzes were inlaid with precious metals, such as gold and silver, depicting scenes from history, ritual ceremonies, and legends.

Pottery continued to be the main material from which everyday items were made. In the later Han dynasty, glazed pottery and porcelain began to be used. Clay was used to make models of people, animals, and houses.

Painting, mostly on silk, was highly developed, and the subjects included humans and landscapes. Tomb paintings from the Han dynasty show scenes depicting human figures and landscapes.

▶ The First Paper

Ancient China's greatest contribution to world culture from the period may well be that of paper. Paper was first manufactured and used in ancient China in the first century A.D. and began to be widely used in China by the third or fourth century A.D.[1] It was not until twelve hundred years later that paper was first manufactured in Italy. Its discovery spread from China to Syria, Iraq, and Egypt before making its way to Italy.

GOVERNMENT

The first ruler of the Shang dynasty united a number of kingdoms in 1523 B.C. after years of war. The Shang dynasty was led by a king who ruled through aristocratic families appointed to govern throughout the kingdom. The king was the leader of the armies and also acted as a priest. He was succeeded in rule by his sons or his brothers. The Shang kings waged aggressive wars and expanded their rule by founding new towns as farmers' settlements. Records of government activities from this period come from inscriptions on the divination bones and shells that have been excavated by archaeologists, particularly from one of the Shang capitals at Anyang.

▷ The Zhou Dynasty

Under the Zhou dynasty, which overthrew the Shang in 1027 B.C., kings continued to rule the government, and they were succeeded by their sons. The king, assisted by relatives and aristocratic families, ruled over a population of about 13.7 million. Various regions of the Zhou kingdom were given to individuals to govern. Those people then pledged military support and allegiance to the Zhou king.

The appointment of local rulers led to a growing independence of various regions, and the central government's authority grew less powerful. In the period 771 to 476 B.C., known as the Spring and Autumn period, these regions

had grown to be semi-independent states whose loyalty to the Zhou king was not nearly as great as it had once been.[1]

From 475 B.C. to 221 B.C., although the Zhou kings remained in power, these regions were constantly at war with each other. This period in Chinese history is known as the Warring States period.

The Qin Dynasty Unites the Empire

The chaos and constant warfare of the Warring States period ended in 221 B.C., when the rulers of the Zhou dynasty as well as the various states were conquered and overthrown by the Qin dynasty. It was with the Qin dynasty that China's centralized form of government

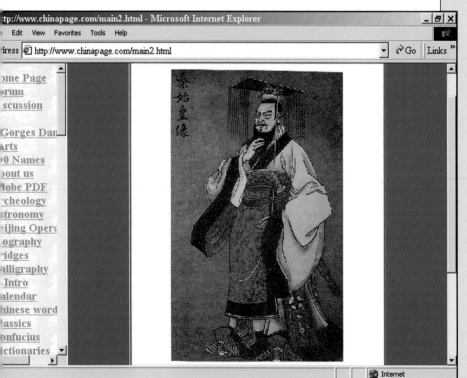

This painting offers one representation of the "First Emperor" of China, the Qin emperor Shi Huangdi.

41

began. The Qin dynasty was founded by Shi Huangdi, known as the First Emperor. He was assisted by a minister, Li Si, who followed the theories of Legalism to build a strong centralized state under the emperor's rule.

However, while the principles of Legalism exerted the greatest influence under the First Emperor, Confucianism and Taoism continued to exist. The First Emperor was particularly interested in the mystical elements of Taoism, particularly the theory that certain magic potions might give him immortality, or everlasting life.[2]

The First Emperor and Li Si set about unifying the new empire. They divided it into thirty-six regions called commanderies. Each region was governed by officials who were appointed by the central government, which was based in the capital of the empire. This system of government was greatly expanded in the Han dynasty. There, three senior officials were put in charge of nine ministers, each heading a different ministry. These senior officials were assisted by large staffs of assistants, clerks, and advisors.[3]

▶ Standardized Writing and Coins

One of the most important changes made by the First Emperor was the standardization of the written language. At the time of the First Emperor's conquest, written Chinese consisted of many different languages and dialects. The dialects were so different from each other that people in one region often could not understand the writings of people from another region. By developing a standard form of writing, the ruler of the Qin dynasty ensured that the written word would have the same meaning throughout the vast reaches of his empire, although the spoken dialects of China have remained varied throughout its history. Weights

The construction of the Great Wall was begun during the Qin dynasty. Although it could not entirely keep out invading armies, its symbolism and importance to the Chinese people has endured for centuries.

and measurements as well as coins were also standardized in this period.

The government also melted down all weapons not used for battle, and the metal was used to make statues and memorials to the First Emperor. The ancient walls around selected cities and towns that had separated them were torn down. Roads and canals were built, further unifying the empire. Even the width of the axles of the carts that traveled these new roads was fixed by the government.

The Great Wall Begins

In the north, the many defensive walls built as early as 300 B.C. began to be connected. This project was the beginning of what would much later become the Great Wall of China. It was built to keep out northern invaders and mark the northern border of the empire.

▷ Pain and Progress

Despite the things he accomplished during his rule, the First Emperor was also known for the harsh treatment that people received during his years in power. To further unify the empire and crush all his opponents, he destroyed thousands of historical records and books, except for scientific texts and certain religious texts. No one was allowed to oppose his will. One hundred and twenty thousand of the leading families in the empire were forced to move to the capital. In one of his most brutal acts, he ordered 460 opponents of his regime to be executed by burning them or burying them alive.

The basic form of government that was established by the First Emperor and Li Si would remain in existence until the revolution of 1911, when China became a republic. But the First Emperor's dynasty was ended by popular rebellion in the third year of the reign of his youngest son, who succeeded him.

▷ The Han Dynasty

The Han dynasty, which followed the Qin dynasty, was influenced by the doctrine of Legalism. Its rulers kept and expanded the strong central government that had begun under Shi Huangdi's rule. The Han emperors also favored Taoism, but they adopted Confucianism as the official state philosophy. Unlike the First Emperor, Shi Huangdi, the emperors of the Han dynasty allowed other philosophies and ideas, particularly Taoism, to be practiced.[4]

Through conquest and natural growth, China's population under the Han dynasty soared. In 2 B.C., as the Western Han dynasty was approaching its end, the government census showed that the population of the empire was 59.6 million in 12.2 million households.

Chapter Notes

Chapter 1. An Army Protects the First Emperor

1. Jane O'Connor, *The Emperor's Silent Army* (New York: Penguin Group, 2002), p. 30.

2. J.A.G. Roberts, *A Concise History of China* (Cambridge, Mass.: Harvard University Press, 1999), p. 25.

Chapter 2. History

1. Dun J. Li, *The Ageless Chinese: A History* (New York: Charles Scribner's Sons, 1965), p. 45.

2. Ibid., pp. 103–104.

Chapter 3. Land, People, and Religion

1. W. Scott Morton, *China: Its History and Culture* (New York: Lippincott & Crowell, 1980), p. 6.

2. Dun J. Li, *The Ageless Chinese: A History* (New York: Charles Scribner's Sons, 1965), p. 8.

3. L. Carrington Goodrich, *A Short History of the Chinese People* (New York: Harper & Row, 1963), p. 17.

4. Morton, p. 18.

5. Ibid., p. 31.

6. John King Fairbank, *China: A New History* (Cambridge, Mass.: The Belknap Press of Harvard University Press, 1992), p. 37.

7. Wolfram Eberhard, *A History of China* (Berkeley and Los Angeles: University of California Press, 1969), p. 22.

8. Ibid., p. 23.

9. Jacques Gernet, *A History of Chinese Civilization* (New York: Cambridge University Press, 1982), p. 91.

10. Leslie Stevenson and David L. Haberman, *Ten Theories of Human Nature* (New York: The Oxford University Press, 1998), pp. 26–27.

11. Ibid., p. 27.

12. Ibid., p. 35.

13. Ibid., p. 36.

14. Li, p. 85.

15. Lao Tzu, *Tao Te Ching: Translated with an introduction by D. C. Lau* (London, Great Britain: Penguin Books, 1963), p. viii.

16. Ibid., p. xxv.

Chapter 4. Family Life: Education, Food, Clothing, Shelter

1. Jacques Gernet, *A History of Chinese Civilization* (New York: Cambridge University Press, 1982), p. 133.

2. Michael Loewe and Edward L. Shaughnessy, *The Cambridge History of Ancient China From the Origins of Civilization to 221 B.C.* (New York: Cambridge University Press, 1999), p. 455.

3. "3,000-Year-Old Food for Thought," *China Daily*, March 13, 2003, <http://www.china.org.cn/english/culture/58121.htm> (November 20, 2003).

4. L. Carrington Goodrich, *A Short History of the Chinese People* (New York: Harper & Row, 1963), p. 51.

5. Kenneth Scott Latourette, *The Chinese: Their History and Culture* (New York: Macmillan, 1962), p. 661.

Chapter 5. Arts and Cultural Contributions

1. Michael Loewe and Edward L. Shaughnessy, *The Cambridge History of Ancient China From the Origins of Civilization to 221 B.C.* (New York: Cambridge University Press, 1999), p. 650.

Chapter 6. Government

1. L. Carrington Goodrich, *A Short History of the Chinese People* (New York: Harper & Row, 1963), pp. 19–21.

2. Michael Loewe & Edward L. Shaughnessy, *The Cambridge History of Ancient China From the Origins of Civilization to 221 B.C.* (New York: Cambridge University Press, 1999), p. 78.

3. Ibid., p. 1,017.

4. Dun J. Li, *The Ageless Chinese: A History* (New York: Charles Scribner's Sons, 1965), p. 115.

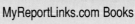

Further Reading

Baldwin, Robert F. *Daily Life in Ancient and Modern Beijing.* Minneapolis: Runestone Press, 1999.

Beshore, George. *Science in Ancient China.* Danbury, Conn.: Scholastic Library Publishing, 1998.

Collier, Irene Dea. *Chinese Mythology.* Berkeley Heights, N.J.: Enslow Publishers, Inc., 2001.

Cotterell, Arthur. *Ancient China.* New York: Knopf, 1994.

Dunshea, Chris. *Cambridge Junior History: Ancient and Medieval China.* New York: Cambridge University Press, 2001.

Guile, Melanie. *China.* Chicago: Raintree, 2004.

Hall, Eleanor J. *Ancient Chinese Dynasties.* San Diego: Lucent Books, 2000.

Jian, Li. *The Glory of the Silk Road: Art from Ancient China.* Dayton, Ohio: Dayton Art Institute, 2003.

O'Connell, Kim A. *China: A MyReportLinks.com Book.* Berkeley Heights, N.J.: Enslow Publishers, Inc., 2004.

Tracy, Kathleen. *The Life and Times of Confucius.* Newark, Del.: Mitchell Lane Publishers, Inc., 2004.

Woods, Michael, and Mary B. Woods. *Ancient Construction: From Tents to Towers.* Minneapolis: Runestone Press, 2000.

A
Anyang, 40
art, 38–39

D
development of calendar, 32–33
development of paper, 39

E
education, 37

F
family life, 32–37

G
geography
  East China Sea, 20
  Kunlun Mountains, 20
  Li River, 30
  South China Sea, 20
  Tibetan plateau, 21
  Yangzi River (Chang Jiang), 20–22
  Yellow River (Huang He), 20–22
  Yellow Sea, 20–21
government, 17, 23, 40–44
Great Wall of China, 18, 43–44

H
Han dynasty, 16–19, 22, 26, 27, 32, 44

I
industry, 22–23, 30–34

L
Liu Pang, 16

M
Mongolia, Mongols, 17, 18

P
Philosophy and religion
  Analects, 28
  ancestor worship, 24
  Book of Changes, 30
  Confucius/Confucianism, 19, 26, 27–30, 31, 37, 42
  Daodejing (Lao Zi), 31
  Lao Zi/Taoism, 19, 26, 30–31, 42
  Legalism, 19, 26–27, 42
  Mencius, 30
  Shangdi ("Lord Most High"), 24
  Wu Jing, 29

Q
Qin dynasty, 12, 15–16, 18–19, 23, 24, 26, 32, 35, 41–42
Qing dynasty, 12

S
Shaanxi province, 10
Shang dynasty, 12, 13–14, 22, 23, 24, 25, 32, 35, 40
Shi Huangdi, First Emperor, 11–12, 15, 18, 25, 42, 44
silk, 20, 33–34
Spring and Autumn period, 14, 40–41
standardized writing, 15

T
terra-cotta warriors, 10–12

W
Wang Mang, 17, 32–33
Warring States period, 14, 35, 41

X
Xia dynasty, 12, 13
Xi'an, 10

Z
Zhou dynasty, 12, 13–14, 25, 27, 32, 33, 40–41